SUFFOLK
PUB WALKS

Laurie Page

COUNTRYSIDE BOOKS
NEWBURY BERKSHIRE

COUNTRYSIDE BOOKS
3 Catherine Road
Newbury, Berkshire

To view our complete range of books,
please visit us at
www.countrysidebooks.co.uk

ISBN 978 1 84674 399 3

All materials used in the manufacture of this book carry FSC certification

Produced by The Letterworks Ltd., Reading
Designed and Typeset by KT Designs, St Helens
Printed by Holywell Press, Oxford

CONTENTS

PUBLISHER'S NOTE

We hope that you obtain considerable enjoyment from this book; great care has been taken in its preparation. Although at the time of publication all routes followed public rights of way or permitted paths, diversion orders can be made and permissions withdrawn.

We cannot, of course, be held responsible for such diversion orders and any inaccuracies in the text which result from these or any other changes to the routes, nor any damage which might result from walkers trespassing on private property. We are anxious though that all the details covering the walks are kept up to date and would therefore welcome information from readers which would be relevant to future editions.

The simple sketch maps that accompany the walks in this book are based on notes made by the author whilst checking out the routes on the ground. They are designed to show you how to reach the start, to point out the main features of the overall circuit and they contain a progression of numbers that relate to the paragraphs of the text.

However, for the benefit of a proper map, we do recommend that you purchase the relevant Ordnance Survey sheet covering your walk. The Ordnance Survey maps are widely available, especially through booksellers and local newsagents.

Area Map showing locations of the walks

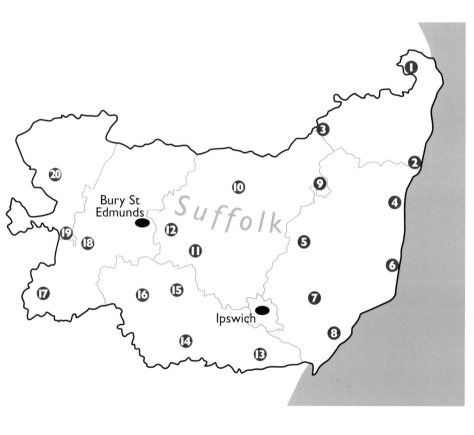

INTRODUCTION

To my mind, there can be no better way to appreciate the beauty of Suffolk than by getting out for a stroll in the countryside and ending up in a cracking local pub. Hopefully, once you've sampled a few of the walks in this book, you'll see just what I mean.

The 20 walks you find here are a gateway to all the things that make Suffolk so special – from rolling farmland and quaint villages to iconic coastal locations and sleepy woodland paths.

Among the villages featured here are picture-postcard spots including Polstead, Chelsworth and Laxfield. There are also walks from the characterful coastal locations of Southwold and Aldeburgh, the amazing historic medieval town of Lavenham, and walks at grand estates near Ickworth House and Somerleyton Hall.

Of course, part of the pleasure in a lengthy stroll is the promise of some refreshment at the end. Each of these routes comes with a recommendation for a pub worthy of the walk itself. One of the perks of the job is getting to test a few of the available establishments. I can assure you if they made it into this book, they fought off some stiff competition.

It's easy to forget, but we really are lucky to have such a vast network of footpaths and public rights of way open every day of the year. The routes I have chosen predominantly use these footpaths but also some of our country lanes, where the footpaths are not available.

I hope you'll get as much enjoyment from taking these walks as I did putting them together. I might even see you out on a path somewhere!

Many thanks go to my brother Martin and his wife Cathy for their contribution to the walk at Hollesley.

Laurie Page

Walk 1
SOMERLEYTON

Distance: 5¼ miles (8.5 km)

Map: OS Explorer OL40 The Broads. **Grid Ref:** TM478971.

How to get there: Take the B1074 which runs between St Olaves and Lowestoft. When you are about two miles south-east of St Olaves, turn right into Slugs Lane. The pub is further down on the right. **Sat Nav:** NR32 5QR.

Parking: Park at the Duke's Head. The owners are happy for walkers to use the pub car park but please ask permission on arrival.

Somerleyton Hall lies close to the Suffolk-Norfolk border and is an impressive stately home which dominates the small pretty village of Somerleyton. The walk goes through the village with its quaint cottages, old school, post office and village green and out into the countryside towards the parish of Blundeston.

Part of the route is along the Angles Way, a long-distance footpath running for 93 miles between Great Yarmouth and Thetford.

THE PUB THE DUKE'S HEAD is a friendly, privately-owned freehouse dating from the early 19th century. It was once two houses

which were knocked into one to become a pub. It has a very large garden overlooking fields and a play area for children. The menu is seasonal, and much of the fresh, local ingredients are sourced from the Somerleyton Estate or surrounding farms. Open every day from 12 noon.

⊕ somerleyton.co.uk/the-dukes-head ☎ 01502 730281

The Walk

1 Turn right out of the pub car park and, keeping to the pavement, follow the road which bends left. Pass the village pond and continue along the village road to the main road junction. Go straight on along the pavement past the thatched school. Shortly after the road bends left, at the road junction, go right (crossing the road carefully) signed to **Ashby**. In about ¼ mile, where the long wall ends, turn right into the pedestrian access for **Somerleyton Hall**.

2 Proceed along the track and, before you reach the Hall, look out for a footpath on the left, (go straight on if you wish to visit the Hall). Follow along the edge of a large field with a hedge to the right. When you reach the crossroads of gravel tracks, turn right along a straight dusty track between hedges. Pass through **Kitty's Farm** where the track turns to a grass path running around the field. Continue into the next field, at the end of which the path turns sharp right through the hedgerow and along to **East Wood** where the path swings left alongside trees. Continue on to where you enter a little wood. Emerge

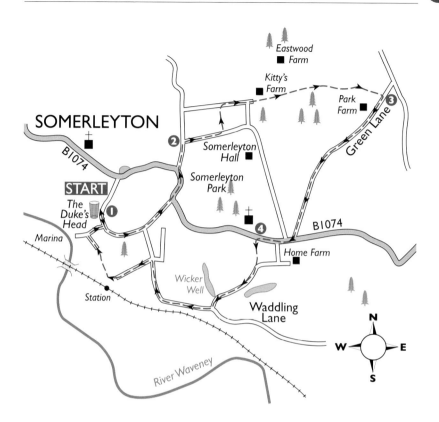

into a field. Bear right through the hedge and across the middle of a crop field to the lane.

③ Turn right along **Green Lane**. Pass **Park Farm** and, further along on the left, you pass **Green Farm**. Continue all the way to the end of the lane. At the main road turn right, passing the main entrance to Somerleyton Hall. Keep to the verge. There is a good view of the church to the right. After the road bends right, look out for a stile concealed in the hedge on the left.

④ Take this footpath alongside the crop field. At the end, go straight ahead onto a wide unmade track. Proceed to the end at the junction where it joins **Waddling Lane**. Turn right along **Angles Way**. Continue along a shady path to a footpath junction where you bear right uphill to the road by the farm. Turn left

(Angles Way) along the lane. At the junction at the end, turn right onto a raised path. Bear right at the next junction past the ancient **Somerleyton Brick Kiln**. At the **Marina** junction, turn right going uphill until you reach the road. The **Duke's Head** can be seen to your left.

Places of Interest

There has been a house on the site of **Somerleyton Hall** since the 13th century, but the current house and garden owes its appearance to the business entrepreneur and Member of Parliament, Sir Samuel Morton Peto, Baronet, who purchased the house in 1843. Peto famously also managed the construction firms that built Nelson's Column and the new Houses of Parliament which made him his fortune. In 1863, Somerleyton Hall was sold to the Crossley family, well-known carpet manufacturers, and today is still owned by the 4th Baron Somerleyton, Hugh Crossley. The house is open to the public from April to October and the gardens have a yew hedge maze, a walled garden, an aviary and a large pergola.
⊕ somerleyton.co.uk/somerleyton-hall

Walk 2
SOUTHWOLD

Distance: 4¼ miles (7 km)

Map: OS Explorer 231 Southwold & Bungay
Grid Ref: TM496755.

How to get there: Turn off the A12 just north of Blythburgh onto the A1095 which takes you directly into Southwold. Turn right into York Road and go all the way to the quayside at the end. Sat Nav: IP18 6TA.

Parking: Parking is free on the quayside in and around the front of the pub.

Southwold is a lovely seaside resort with charming beach huts, a lighthouse and a pier. This coastal walk takes you around the town and by the tidal River Blyth. You'll explore the marshes on a raised path, then stroll along the seafront on the Suffolk Coast Path before returning beside the river which divides Southwold from Walberswick.

THE PUB THE HARBOUR INN is an old sailors' and fishermen's pub with low ceiling beams, a cosy interior, and a nautical theme. There is outside seating at the front of the pub where you can view the boats on the River Blyth or you can choose from the back terrace or spacious garden overlooking the Suffolk countryside. Dogs and children are welcome. ⊕ harbourinnsouthwold.co.uk ☎ 01502 722381

The Walk

1 From the quayside in front of the pub, go right and follow the gravel path that runs along by the **River Blyth**. This soon becomes a raised path with a lovely view of Southwold and its lighthouse to the right. Pass the **Bailey Bridge** which connects to the village of **Walberswick** and continue straight on, going through a metal gate. The path bends away from the river. At the weir keep straight on along the raised path. This bends left then soon after right. Eventually you pass through a metal cattle gate then a wooden gate to a footpath crossroads.

2 Proceed straight on over a little wooden bridge and alongside a

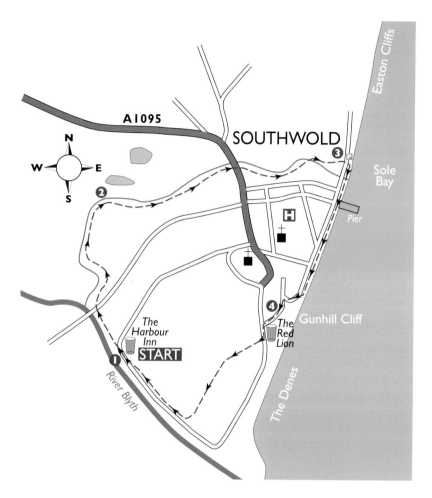

water channel to your left. Continue on and **Southwold church** comes into view. When you reach the main road (**Mights Road**), cross carefully and take the footpath opposite, at first through the trees and then grassland. Continue for some distance towards the beach huts.

3 Just before the beach car park, go right along the field. At the end of the field, go out to your left along the promenade which takes you past the pier. Then, you can choose the beach path or the cliff path, a little higher that runs parallel. Continue past

the lighthouse. Turn right into **East Street** then left at **Pinkneys Lane**. At the next junction turn left into **Queen Street**.

4 Pass the **Red Lion** and follow the path by the postbox along the raised terrace. As you descend to the road junction (**Gardner Road**) take the footpath on the right along a wide stony track. Soon, there is a seat on the left. Follow this path all the way to the riverbank where you can see Walberswick on the other side of the water. Turn right, passing the ferry and continue along the stony boat path back to the **Harbour Inn**.

Places of Interest

The seaside resort of Southwold is one of the most popular seaside resorts in Suffolk. It has beaches and beach huts, a busy pier and its magnificent lighthouse (the town's trademark). You can tour the **Adnams Brewery** which supplies many of the pubs featured in this book. Southwold is an old fashioned town which is what gives it its charm. There are quaint shops and tearooms along the main street and an unusual amber shop and museum which is the largest and oldest of its kind in the UK and definitely worth a visit. You can take the ferry to **Walberswick Harbour** or go via the Bailey Bridge which you pass on your walk.

Walk 3
HOMERSFIELD

Distance: 4½ miles (7.2 km)

Map: OS Explorer 231 Southwold & Bungay.
Grid Ref: TM283856.

How to get there: Take the B1062 from Bungay which goes directly into the village of Homersfield. Alternatively, take the A143 from Harleston and turn off onto the B1062. The Black Swan is in Church Lane at the north end of the village. **Sat Nav:** IP20 0ET.

Parking: There is good parking in and around the Black Swan.

The village of Homersfield lies close to the county border between Suffolk and Norfolk, the two counties separated by the River Waveney. Crossing the river is the Homersfield Bridge, a stone's throw from the start of the walk, which is the oldest reinforced concrete bridge in Britain, constructed in 1869. The

route passes sand and gravel pits, some converted into lakes, and takes you to the parish of St Cross South Elmham. The return leg is along lanes and part of the Angles Way, by Limbourne Common.

THE PUB THE BLACK SWAN is a family-run pub dating from 1783. It has four separate areas including a restaurant section serving home-made food. There is an open fire, and unusually, an aquarium inside. Outside there is further seating in a pretty, secluded garden.

⊕ blackswanhomersfield.co.uk ☎ 01986 788204

The Walk

❶ From the pub entrance go left up to the road junction. Turn left again past the play area and Barnfield thatched cottages. At the next junction keep right and walk along the verge of the main road. Pass a road junction and watch out for fast moving traffic, especially on this last section where there is little verge. After about 150 metres, turn right onto a bridleway. At the next junction, go left along a wide track, passing a lake to the left. After the gravel and sand pit, at a junction of tracks, turn right. Continue gently uphill along the track. This bends right at **Home Farm**. Proceed ahead to the lane (**Park Road**) at **Chestnut Tree Farm**.

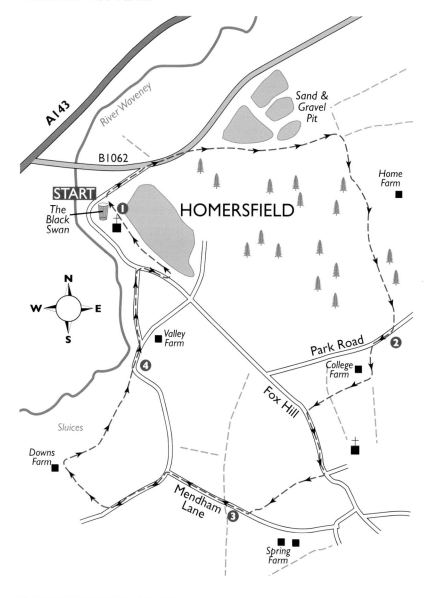

The unusual village sign, known locally as the 'Totem Pole', which was carved by local artist Mark Goldsworthy. The inscription reads 'I dreamed of a beautiful woman who carried me away'. This is thought to be a reference to when the River Waveney, which flows past the village, was called 'Alveron' meaning 'beautiful woman'.

2 Turn right along the lane. Then take the next unsigned footpath on the left by the oak tree, to **College Farm**. At the farm cross a stile and turn right between brick barns. Proceed straight on into the next field where you get a view of the church to your left. When you reach the lane (**Fox Hill**), turn left. Opposite the entrance to the church take the footpath on the right, through a meadow. Go through a gate and down steps and through the trees. Emerge into the open where the path swings right along by a large crop field. At the end you join the lane (**Mendham Lane**).

3 Bear right along the lane and continue to the road junction. Go left and at the next little crossroads, turn right along a hard surfaced track going down to a junction of paths at **Downs Farm**. Take the path straight ahead, the **Angles Way**. Go over a high stile and bear right along the field edge on a bank following the fence. Negotiate another stile and walk on through trees by a stream. This path winds through the woods for just over ¼ mile and eventually joins the road.

4 Turn left and at the road junction in 200 metres, go left again along a narrow lane. At the end turn right, and where the road bends right, turn left onto a bridleway. This takes you past the church where the route converts to a hard surface, coming out at the children's play area. Turn left then immediately right to return to the pub.

Places of Interest

At Flixton, two miles to the north-east of Homersfield, is the **Norfolk and Suffolk Aviation Museum** which lies next to one of Suffolk's World War Two airfields. Opened in 1975, it is run by volunteers and relies on donations and grants. There are over 60 historic aircraft and many different artefacts and photographs including areas dedicated to Air Sea Rescue, RAF Bomber Command, Flight Training and Royal Observer Corps. Admission is free. ⊕ aviationmuseum.net

Walk 4
EASTBRIDGE & RSPB MINSMERE

Distance: 5 miles (8 km)

Map: OS Explorer 212 Woodbridge & Saxmundham.
Grid Ref: TM452661.

How to get there: From the B1122 between Leiston and Yoxford take the turning 2 miles north of Leiston into Onners Lane. Keep straight on into the village and the Eel's Foot Inn is on the right.
Sat Nav: IP16 4SN.

Parking: There is a large car park at the Eel's Foot.

On the east coast, south of Dunwich, is RSPB Minsmere with its lagoons, heath and woodland. This walk, from the little village of Eastbridge, circumnavigates the nature reserve where you will also see the familiar dome of Sizewell B nuclear power station before walking along part of the Suffolk Coast Path and up to the visitor centre at Coastguard Cottages. Here you can spend some time before returning to the village via further heathland and woodland.

THE PUB THE EEL'S FOOT INN is very popular and gets good reviews. There is accommodation, an extensive menu and all the best Adnams ales from the brewery up the road at Southwold. Produce is mainly from local suppliers and fresh fish is delivered daily from Lowestoft. The terraced garden has plenty of seating, a children's play area and a barbeque in the summer. Inside there is a restaurant and a log burner for colder days.

🌐 theeelsfootinn.co.uk ☎ 01728 830154

The Walk

❶ Turn left out of the pub and walk up the lane. After **Rose Cottage**, take the footpath on the left along a stony drive. Turn immediately right along by the barbed wire fence and then out into fields. In ¼ mile go through a pedestrian gate and continue for a further ¼ mile. Go through a kissing gate and then keep to the main track for ¾ mile. Pass the ruins of an old chapel (belonging to **Leiston Abbey**). The familiar landmark of the Sizewell nuclear power station dome can be seen to the right. Eventually you reach the coastal path.

❷ Turn left. There are two paths running parallel to choose from. The lower path is wider, straighter and easy to walk but the narrower raised path, which meanders through the sand dunes, has lovely sea views. Head for the white building in the distance, which is one of two visitor centres. Continue for almost a mile. (Ignore the first turning to the visitor centre which is not the white building ahead.) To the left are the hides and lagoons of **RSPB Minsmere**. Eventually the two paths converge near the beach along a stony track. Keep to the left and take the path through a gate with a fence to the right. At the T-junction go

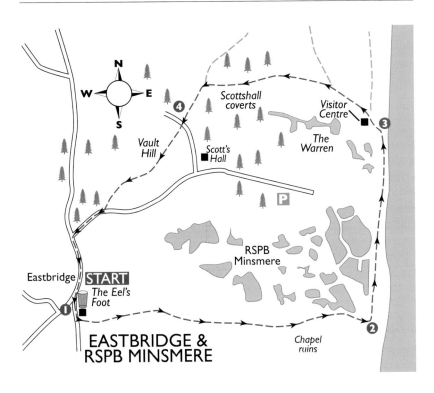

EASTBRIDGE &
RSPB MINSMERE

right, then immediately left onto a bridleway taking you to the visitor centre car park.

3 You may wish to spend time at the visitor centre (see *Places of Interest* on p23). To continue, go around the car park to the left. Pass the toilet block and take the public footpath on the left by **Heath Barn**. At the fork, take the left path going through the fields of heather. Keep straight on until you reach a footpath junction where there is a bench and a kissing gate to the left of the track. Go through the kissing gate and up through the trees. The path swings left and passes a woodland information board. Follow this for around ¾ mile until you reach the road (which leads to the visitor centre).

4 Go straight over going gently uphill into heathland. Pass two seats then continue back into woodland. Go downhill to join the road where you go straight on. The road swings left and then crosses a road bridge. Cross another smaller bridge and the **Eel's Foot** is a little further along on the left.

Places of Interest

RSPB Minsmere is home to a huge variety of birds including rare breeds such as the avocet, bittern and marsh harrier. Mammals such as otters, voles, red deer and badger, as well as fish and an abundance of different insect varieties can also be seen. There are eight hides and two visitor centres with a café, shop and toilets.
⊕ rspb.org.uk

Walk 5

KETTLEBURGH

Distance: 4 miles (6.4 km)

Map: OS Explorer 212 Woodbridge & Saxmundham.
Grid Ref: TM263600.

How to get there: From the A1120 between Yoxford and Stowmarket turn off at Earl Soham south, going through Brandeston. Kettleburgh is the next village. After the first junction the pub is on the right. From the A12 turn off at Wickham Market and follow the road via Easton. **Sat Nav:** IP13 7JT.

Parking: Park at the Chequers Inn. If this is full you can try the village hall a bit further along the route (*see below*).

Kettleburgh is a small village comprising a few houses, a church, a pub, a village hall, and green. This is a lovely country walk from the little community at Kettleburgh through the parishes of Easton and Hoo. There is very little traffic along the quiet lanes and you may complete the whole route without seeing another person along the way!

THE PUB THE CHEQUERS INN has had a chequered history! It has burnt down on more than one occasion, the last time in 1812, which is when the current building dates from. It is a freehouse with a small restaurant area and two bar sections.
At the back of the building there is a large patio area with bench seating and alongside it, more unusually, a pétanque court (boules or bowls) where local teams compete.
⊕ thechequers.net ☎ 01728 723760

The Walk

1 From the pub turn left along the road and at the road junction turn right (to **Framlingham**). Pass the village sign. At the village hall, turn right up the track, then right again the other

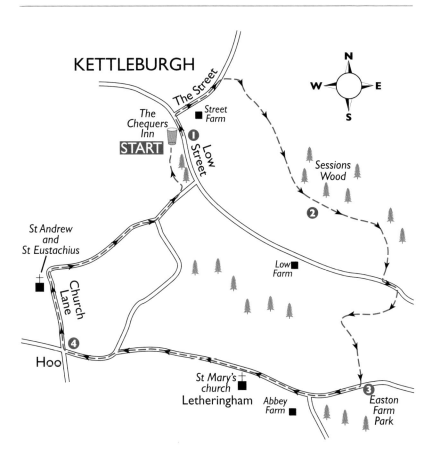

side of the house, onto a grass path. This takes you up by the horse paddocks. At the top go through a gap to the right and bear left along the edge of a large field with distant views of the surrounding countryside. Continue to follow the route alongside a ditch. Cross a little planked bridge at the end of the field and proceed past Sessions Wood which is to your left.

2 The path continues around an S bend and alongside a high hedge to your left. Cross over a footbridge and keep ahead past another wood to the left. At the end of the wood, by the footpath junction, take the right fork. Go gently uphill and continue to the road. Turn left along the road for a short distance and take the next footpath on the right. Keep the hedge to your right. The path swings right into the next field. Go downhill to the end of the field and turn left alongside a concealed stream. Proceed along the field boundary until you reach the lane.

3 Turn right along the lane. (For the entrance to **Easton Farm Park** go left.) The church comes into view. Cross a stream and continue past the church. Go all the way to the end of the road to the junction where there is a seat for a rest. Bear left along the road and watch out for traffic. At the next road junction go right and then immediately right again into **Church Lane**. This is a

long straight lane which leads to **St Andrew and St Eustachius Church** in **Hoo**.

4 Pass the church and in 100 metres, the lane bends sharp right. Go all the way to the end where, at the T-junction, you turn left. After you cross the road bridge, turn left onto a footpath. Go past the house and through the gate to the right of the one that says 'private' going between hedges. Pass through two more gates and soon you will arrive at the **Chequers** pub car park.

Places of Interest

Easton Farm Park was owned by the Duke of Hamilton in the 19th century and many of the Victorian buildings survive today. When the working farm became redundant in the 1970s, it became a farm park for families to enjoy. There is a blacksmith's forge with a resident blacksmith, the Victorian dairy, a café, a shop and you can feed the animals, including the Suffolk Punch horses which also give horse and cart rides.
⊕ eastonfarmpark.co.uk

Walk 6
ALDEBURGH

Distance: 4 miles (6.3 km)

Map: OS Explorer 212 Woodbridge & Saxmundham.
Grid Ref: TM464559.

How to get there: Turn off the A12 south of Saxmundham onto the A1094. This will take you directly into Aldeburgh. Turn right at the seafront and go all the way through the town to the end at Slaughden Quay where there is a large free car parking area on your left. **Sat Nav:** IP15 5DE.

Parking: Fort Green Car Park, Brudenell Street.

Aldeburgh is an old fashioned seaside town of character, where you'll find art galleries, Victorian and Edwardian buildings and traditional fish and chip shops. This walk goes from the coast at the south end of the town, along by the River Alde from where the town gets its name, and back via the Aldeburgh marshes. Along the route, is England's largest surviving Martello Tower, built to stop a potential invasion from the French under Napoleon's rule. It is essentially four towers joined together and located on a narrow spit of land along the coast between the sea and the River Alde. The tower remains in fantastic condition and has been converted into a house.

THE PUB THE BRUDENELL is a hotel situated right in front of the beach with views overlooking the sea. It is open all day every day and serves food from breakfast early in the morning through to evening meals. You can sit on the terrace at the front and order food and drinks while you watch the seafront activity on and off the water. The restaurant specialises in seafood, with fresh fish caught locally.

⊕ brudenellhotel.co.uk ☎ 01728 452071

The Walk

1 From the car park, head back towards the town on the approach road to the car park, Take the first turning on the left into **Park Road**. After number 20, turn left onto an unmarked stony track which is a footpath. Swing right then bear left at the metal gate following the waymarker signs. The path passes through reed beds and alongside a water channel. The **Martello Tower** can be seen to the left. The grass path joins a gravel track taking you to steps going up to the sea wall. Turn right through a wooden gate and proceed along the sea wall.

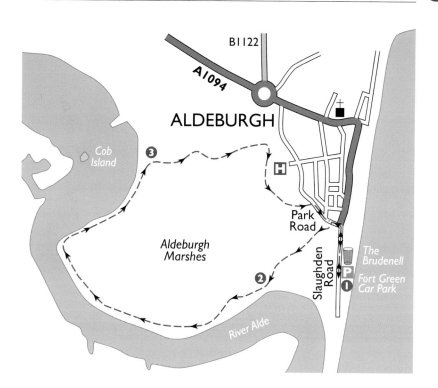

2 Pass through a metal gate. There is a lower path running parallel if you need to be protected from the wind. At the next footpath junction go through the metal gate and continue along by the **River Alde**. The path is on a very gradual long bend to the right. Continue for some distance to the next gate which is **West Row Point**, where the path turns sharp right. Continue along the raised river path for another ½ mile. Eventually, you come to steps going down on the right which is the continuation of the footpath.

3 Follow this path through a gate and going alongside a field. Ahead, in the distance, the **Aldeburgh Victorian water tower** can be seen. Cross a track and go through a double set of gates either side of a footbridge. Proceed across the middle of a field to two more gates, then another grassy meadow to another set of gates and footbridge. Cross the water channel and ditch via two

more bridges. Continue past allotments. At the next gate turn right along a good path with a hard surface (and a bench for a rest). Pass houses and enter the outskirts of the town. At **Park Road** turn right and turn right again at the T-junction taking you back to the car park. If you wish to visit the **Brudenell Hotel**, turn left at the hotel sign.

Places of Interest

Aldeburgh Museum is housed in the beautifully preserved 16th-century Moot Hall building close to the seafront. It was built when Aldeburgh became a prosperous town and was once divided into separate shops on the ground floor and a meeting room on the upper floor, where the council still meet today. The existing fireplace was taken from an old Tudor manor house and installed in 1924. In the museum you can learn all about the history of Aldeburgh from Saxon times, the shipbuilding industry and the Aldeburgh witches! It is open from April to October. ⊕ aldeburghmuseum.org.uk

Walk 7

BROMESWELL & SUTTON HOO

Distance: 5¼ miles (8.5 km)

Map: OS Explorer 212 Woodbridge & Saxmundham.
Grid Ref: TM299501.

How to get there: From the A12 north of Woodbridge, turn onto the A1152 through Melton. Cross Wilford Bridge and turn left at the next roundabout onto Orford Road. The Unruly Pig is ½ mile further along on the left. **Sat Nav:** IP12 2PU.

Parking: The Unruly Pig pub car park.

This interesting walk crosses Bromeswell Heath to the National Trust attraction of Sutton Hoo, the site of two early medieval cemeteries dating from the 6th to 7th centuries. It then follows the River Deben for a short way, opposite the town of Woodbridge before returning by Deben Wood, and back across heathland and a golf course.

THE PUB THE UNRULY PIG is an award-winning traditional 16th-century pub. It has original oak beams and a log burner for colder days. For warmer weather there is a decked area for al fresco drinking and dining. It prides itself on its excellent food and good service and is dog friendly.
⊕ theunrulypig.co.uk ☎ 01394 460310

The Walk

1 Take the bridleway opposite the pub, going up a bank and along a grass track next to the golf course. Cross a track by the second tee and fairway to join a gravel track going through the trees. Keep left at the fork and again at the next one, then cross the next

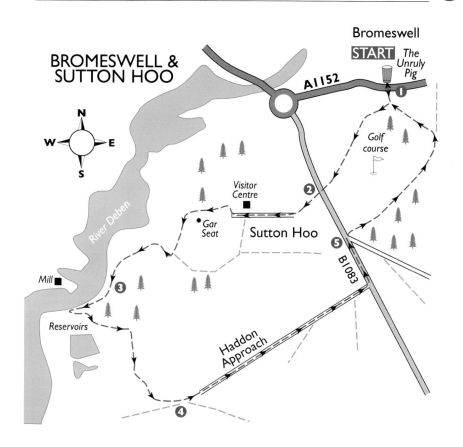

fairway. Join another track and as this bends left, go straight on following a waymarker across the next fairway and alongside the 6th tee, into the trees. Walk past houses then continue along an unmade access road to the main road.

❷ Take the footpath just to the right on the other side of the road. Keep ahead by the edge of a wood next to a wire fence to join a long straight lane. At the end, go straight on at the visitor centre (which you may wish to visit), then go left along a dusty track, taking you to the **Sutton Hoo Burial Ground**. Pass the **Gar Seat**. Go through a gate onto a track and turn right along the track. To the left is the famous **Sutton Hoo mound**. At the fork, go right, going downhill. At **Little Sutton Hoo House**, as the path bends

right, take the footpath at the second exit on the left passing **Dairy Farm Cottage**. Pass a pond and horse paddock and continue to the raised bank by the river.

3 Turn left and proceed along a winding and undulating path running parallel with the **River Deben**, passing over several little bridges. Across the water, is the town of **Woodbridge** and its **Tide Mill**. Go up steps and then the route hairpins sharp left going along by a field. It then swings right then left, joining a sandy track running along by a huge meadow. Further along you are guided right with trees to your left. At the end go straight ahead across a crop field and at the little lane, go left (it is a bridleway) until you reach a junction of tracks.

4 Bear left onto the long, straight lane (**Haddon Approach**). Go all the way (over a mile) to the end passing a pig farm. Just before the main road, turn left onto a path between trees which runs parallel with the road.

5 At the end turn right to the road junction and take the restricted byway ahead, onto a wide track. This converts to a footpath. Stick to the main path and continue to a little car parking area where you go straight ahead onto a wide track through the trees. Continue on past the golf course with trees to the right. Where the track runs out by the white bungalow up to the right, with the fairway in front of you, bear slightly left under the telegraph wires and head for the black and yellow post and the grass path beyond going between the gorse bushes to the next fairway. Bear left again going across the fairway where you will see a waymarker post. Follow the bridleway sign along a good track past an old oak. Keep straight on past the sand store and the track then bends right to a junction. Go right to a cottage by the road. When you reach the road you will see the **Unruly Pig** opposite.

Places of Interest

Sutton Hoo is described as one of the greatest archaeological discoveries in Britain. It is the 7th-century burial place of the Saxon king, Raedwald. Amongst the early finds were the remains of a Saxon ship in which the king was buried with many treasures, most of which are now in the British Museum, including the Sutton Hoo Helmet, a ceremonial headdress of bronze and iron. Sutton Hoo was first discovered in 1939 and in 1998 it was given to the National Trust. ⊕ nationaltrust.org.uk/sutton-hoo

Across the River Deben is **Woodbridge Tide Mill**, a Grade I listed building and one of only two working tide mills in the country. Dating from 1793, it is open to the public from March to October when you can watch the mill wheel turning. ⊕ woodbridgetidemill.org.uk

Walk 8
HOLLESLEY

Distance: 5½ miles (8.7 km)

Map: OS Explorer 197 Ipswich & Felixstowe.
Grid Ref: TM353446.

How to get there: From the B1083 which runs south from Woodbridge to Bawdsey, turn off at Shottisham onto the Hollesley Road. Continue to Bushey Lane and at the T-junction turn left. The pub is about half a mile up on the left in the village centre. Sat Nav: IP12 3QU.

Parking: The Shepherd and Dog Inn is happy for walkers to leave their car in the car park while they walk but please let the landlord know.

Hollesley is a little village close to the North Sea. This walk runs from the village to the coast, along the attractive beach at Shingle Street and back via Oxley Marshes where you're likely to see birds of prey, wading birds, owls, butterflies and dragonflies depending on the time of year. The return leg also passes the prominent landmarks of Martello Towers built at the beginning of the 19th century in defence against a possible French invasion.

THE PUB THE SHEPHERD AND DOG INN is the only pub in the village and is popular with locals and walkers. Locally brewed beers are served along with good quality traditional pub grub. There is a cosy log fire inside and a nice beer garden outside for warmer days. Open from midday every day.

⊕ facebook.com/shepherdanddoghollesley ☎ 01394 411855

The Walk

1 Turn left from the pub car park and then turn almost immediately right up a paved footpath with hedging on the right (not signposted) opposite **Shepherds Fold**. Continue to the end of the footpath to the lane (**Rectory Road**) and turn right, continuing

along the lane, passing a distant view of **Hollesley church** on your right. At the road junction continue straight ahead along the No Through Road, signposted **Shingle Street**, passing fields on both sides. Follow the lane for ½ mile as it swings right.

2 The road then bends sharp left past a cottage. Distant views of the sea can be seen ahead. Cross the road bridge over the water and then turn left at the footpath sign onto a raised path and continue across the marshland towards the coast. At the coast, views of **Orford Ness** can be seen to your left.

3 Turn right and continue along the embankment with the shingle beach and sea to your left. At the end of the embankment, turn right and walk along the beach in front of a row of cottages

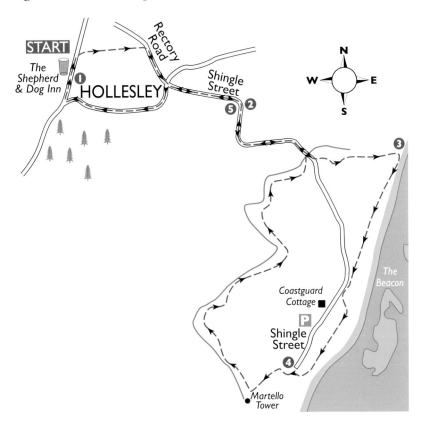

and **HM Coastguard**. Continue along the shingle and grass, passing more cottages until you reach a byway sign where you turn right.

④ Just after the telephone box and the **Shingle Street information board**, turn left towards the **Martello Tower** and then right at the footpath sign, just before the tower. Walk through the trees and follow the path as it bears left and then right, with views of two more Martello Towers in the distance. At the T-junction, turn right, heading away from the towers and continue along the raised path through marshland, passing **Oxley Marsh Sluice** 2 and 1, until you reach a metal gate. Turn right up to the road, and then left, to retrace your steps back across the road bridge over the water and continue along the road, bearing left and back up to the road junction.

5 Turn left, signposted **Alderton** and **Bawdsey**, following the road (**Schools Lane**) past **Moors Farm** and **All Saints Church**, Hollesley (open daily) until you reach the main road. Turn right up the hill and back to the pub on your left.

Places of Interest

When Napoleon was at the height of his powers at the beginning of the 19th century, England feared a French invasion. As a result, round defensive towers were built all along the south and east coast, three of which can be seen on this walk. These brick towers, built between 1808 and 1812, are about 40 feet high with a gun platform on the top, and once housed up to 24 men. Many of the towers have survived and been converted to private residences, others are open to the public or can be rented as a holiday home, such as the one at **Bawdsey** a little further along the coast.

Walk 9

LAXFIELD

Distance: 2¾ miles (4.4 km)

Map: OS Explorer 230 Diss & Harleston. Grid Ref: TM296724.

How to get there: Laxfield lies on the B1117 between Eye and Halesworth. The Royal Oak pub can be found in the centre of the village. Sat Nav: IP13 8DH.

Parking: Park at the Royal Oak.

This lovely route takes you along some quiet lanes which are pleasant and easy to walk, especially in the wet weather. Although this route can be walked any time of year, it would make a good winter walk. Here you'll explore a quiet backwater north of Laxfield village, an area of moated farmhouses and open fields where the views go on for miles.

THE ROYAL OAK is one of two pubs in the village which dates from the 16th century, around the same time as the Guildhall opposite. There are three separate areas inside the pub and a large inglenook fireplace with wooden carvings for colder days. There are also benches outside in the front of the pub where you can watch the comings and goings in the village. The pub is open every day from 10.30 am.

🌐 theroyaloaklaxfield.com ☎ 01986 798666

The Walk

1 From the parking area in front of the **Royal Oak** pub, head uphill past the **Co-op** (also a post office). Cross **Jubilee Close** and just after passing the **Baptist church**, take the footpath on the right just before **The Orchards**. Go along a sandy path, fenced on the left. Cross a footbridge and proceed straight on through some trees and out into a field. At the next footpath junction, go straight on.

2 Continue along the path which follows the field boundary, bordered by a ditch to the right. Go under pylons and pass an old distressed oak tree. At the next waymarker, by the little planked bridge, continue straight on, going gently uphill. At the field end where a ditch runs in front of you, turn left and then right, keeping a ditch to the right. This takes you to the lane by the farmhouse.

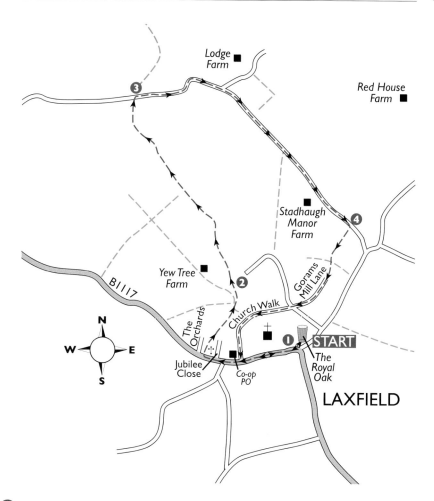

③ Turn right along the lane (**Cake Street**). There are good distant views and **Laxfield church** can be seen to the right. Proceed along the lane for 1 mile. There is very little traffic and a good verge for when any does come along. Pass a farmhouse and go back under the pylons. Pass **Chestnut Farm** and **Moat House**, and then take the next footpath on the right by **Redroofs** bungalow.

④ Follow a stony track which soon narrows to a pleasant grass path. At the bench the church comes into view. Pass allotments. The footpath connects to a stony track where you turn right, going down to the lane (**Gorams Mill Lane**). Turn left along the lane and, in 100 metres, turn right onto the tarmac track (**Church Walk**) going to the right of the church. At the end of this you emerge back into the village centre and the car parking area.

Places of Interest

The attractive, timber-framed **Guildhall** was built between 1515 and 1520 on the site of an earlier hall. A chimney, an attic and the newel stairs were added later. Today it houses **Laxfield & District Museum** where you'll find displays of geology and natural history, along with farm and domestic tools from the local area. The museum started in 1971 as a collection of interesting objects found by the local villagers. Today there is also a Victorian kitchen, a village shop interior and costumes. The museum is open at weekends in the spring and summer. Entrance is free.

Walk 10
THORNHAM MAGNA

Distance: 3 miles (4.8 km)

Map: OS Explorer 230 Diss & Harleston. **Grid Ref:** TM104706.

How to get there: The village of Thornham Magna lies just to the west of the A140, between Yaxley and Stoke Ash. Turn off the A140 into Workhouse Road and the pub is at the junction with The Street and Water Lane. **Sat Nav:** IP23 8HD.

Parking: There is a car park opposite the Four Horseshoes.

This rural walk takes you to the parish of Stoke Ash and along the banks of the River Dove, a tributary of the River Waveney, where you will see cattle grazing on the water meadows. The walk starts near an attractive ford, which can be crossed using a foot bridge and continues across crop fields, returning to Thornham Magna through shady woods and along quiet lanes.

THE PUB THE FOUR HORSESHOES is a large, attractive pink inn with a thatched roof. There is a good atmosphere and this award-winning pub is popular for both food and drink. Inside there are some low beams (watch your head), an open fireplace and a well! There are two function rooms, a large restaurant and bar, and a spacious beer garden.

⊕ thefourhorseshoes.net ☎ 01379 678777

The Walk

① Go down **Water Lane** directly opposite the pub. At the end of this shady lane there is a ford. Rather than getting your feet wet, you can go left over a bridge. Continue up the wide track and past a thatched cottage. Turn left into a large field onto a footpath with a hedge on the left. Follow the wide grass path around the field boundary. This takes you to the main road (A140).

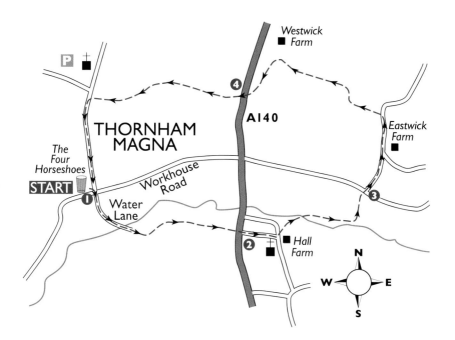

② Cross carefully and take the little lane just to the left (**Church Lane**). Where the lane bends sharp right, go straight on and immediately bear left onto an unmarked footpath between a fence and bushes. Veer a little left onto a wide grass path, crossing a brook. **Stoke Ask church** can be seen to the right. At the path junction keep right alongside a wire fence. At the next path junction, by the double metal gates, turn left along a grass strip between crop fields going gently uphill to the junction at the lane.

③ Go straight ahead along the lane (signed **Braiseworth**). Pass **Eastwick Farm** and **Oly Dale**. Shortly after **Quiet Acres Boarding Kennels**, look out for a footpath through the hedge on the left, going across two large fields. At the oak tree near the end of the second field, follow the path turning left towards the houses and church. Where the field ends, continue along a tarmac track. Pass the chapel to the road.

④ Cross the road with care and turn left, keeping to the pavement.

Take the footpath on the right into a field. Follow a narrow path around the field edge. At the end of the field turn right through a gap in the hedge. Keep straight on by the waymarker post into the next field. Pass a wood on the left then go through a gap on the left and keep right alongside a hedge. At the field end continue into a shady wood and on to the parish hall by the road. Turn left along the lane (or turn right to see the church with some outstanding stained-glass windows). Pass **Lambs Farm**, **The Old Post Office** and other cottages and houses back to the road junction by the pub.

Places of Interest

The ancient market town of **Eye**, which lies a few miles to the north-east of Thornham Magna, became important when the Norman overlord Robert Malet built a castle there. It is still possible to climb to the top of the motte and see the castle ruins on top. A good view of the town can also be seen from here. On a Wednesday, Eye has a country market at the attractive-looking town hall, which has a clock tower and is a listed building.

Walk 11

GREAT FINBOROUGH & BUXHALL

Distance: 3¼ miles (5.2 km)

Map: OS Explorer 211 Bury St Edmunds & Stowmarket.
Grid Ref: TM014577.

How to get there: Head west out of Stowmarket onto the B1115 which leads directly through the village of Great Finborough. The Chestnut Horse lies on the left after Valley Lane. **Sat Nav:** IP14 3AT.

Parking: Walkers can park in the pub car park but please let the proprietor know.

This pleasant walk goes west from Great Finborough to the little community of Buxhall with its windmill and interesting museum (see page 55). You'll walk through crop fields and along quiet country lanes in this unspoilt rural village with distant views and big skies all around, before returning to Great Finborough and a warm welcome at the Chestnut Horse.

THE PUB THE CHESTNUT HORSE was once four old cottages but has been converted into a pub. The main bar area has a fire and a TV screen and there is another small area designated for eating. There are also seats outside to the back but the benches at the front, overlooking the road, offer a more interesting aspect with a view of the pretty cottages and the church. The pub opens seven days a week at 12 noon and food is served every day.
🌐 facebook.com/TheChestnutHorse ☎ 01449 674688

The Walk

1 From the pub, turn left along the pavement on the other side of the road. Just before **Middlefield Drive** take the footpath on the right through a kissing gate. Follow the fence and on the right go through three successive gates through the paddocks. In the far corner of the field, go through a kissing gate and out into an open field. Go straight across heading for the farm buildings and the church in the distance. Descend to reach the end of the field and go straight on over a footbridge then through the middle of a crop field. This swings left under telegraph wires and up to a hedge. Go left to the road.

2 Turn left, then right at the next road junction (**Brettenham Road**) into **Buxhall**. At the next road junction, by **St Mary's Church**, turn left (**Valley Lane**). Go downhill and follow the bend at the bottom. Take the footpath on the right. Cross a footbridge and stile to enter a meadow. Go through a field gate in the far corner and then on the other side of this field cross

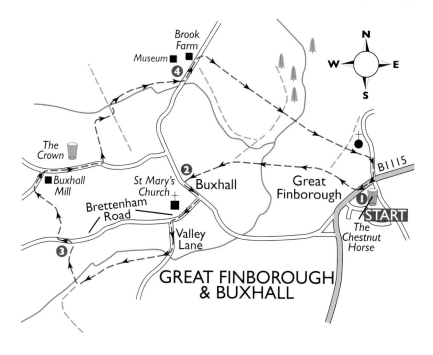

a stile into the next meadow. After another stile you exit this field and go right at the fork and soon after turn right again at the footpath junction. Go around the field boundary to the right, veering left at the field corner. A little further along look out for a little footbridge on the right taking you through a gap in the hedge. Keep right alongside the hedge, going up to the road.

3 Turn left along the lane. Take the next footpath on the right between hedges. This bends sharp left between fences then right to the road by the old chapel (**Mill Road**). Turn right past **Buxhall Mill**. At the road junction, turn right (towards 'Onehouse') past the **Crown** pub. Opposite **Spring Cottage** take the next footpath on the left. Keep to the field, following the hedge. Half way down, go right through a gate and across a grass field. At the footpath T-junction turn left then immediately right along the edge of a large field. At the next junction, go straight on by a ditch and on to the lane.

4 Turn left up the lane. At the top, to visit **Granary Crafts** and see the little museum and gift shop at **Brook Farm**, go left. Otherwise, turn right onto the footpath almost opposite the entrance. This goes into a field and eventually descends into a little wood. Cross a stream via the footbridge and continue into a large field. Go uphill and bear left towards **Great Finborough church** with its magnificent spire. At the footpath

junction by the church keep right by the brick wall, passing the church. This leads to a lane where you turn right. Keep going to reach the road junction with the **Chestnut Horse** pub just to your right.

Places of Interest

Towards the end of the walk is **Granary Crafts** at **Brook Farm**. There is a little gem of a museum showing all sorts of local and bygone items depicting life in Suffolk, including farm equipment, old kitchen implements, toys from the past, and early electrical items such as the first televisions, radios and old gramophones. There are also some vintage Austin cars, a tearoom and souvenir shop. Entrance to the museum is free.

Walk 12
WOOLPIT

Distance: 3 miles (5 km)

Map: OS Explorer 211 Bury St Edmunds & Stowmarket.
Grid Ref: TL974624.

How to get there: Turn off the A14 at junction 47 and follow the signs to Woolpit. As you approach the village there is a car park on the left opposite the parish church. **Sat Nav:** IP30 9QG.

Parking: Village Car Park, a free car park off Church Street opposite the church.

This stroll, from the quaint village of Woolpit, follows a route to the neighbouring parish of Drinkstone with its two windmills and network of footpaths that cross the surrounding arable farmland. The return leg is back via footpaths and quiet country lanes to the centre of Woolpit which is a conservation area and home to many timber-framed buildings.

THE PUB

THE BULL INN is an award-winning pub, restaurant and B&B. You'll find a main bar, pool room and conservatory along with a large beer garden at the back of the building. The menu is made up of traditional pub grub and daily specials, and a good range of real ales and wines are available from the bar. Open daily from 11am.

⊕ bullinnwoolpit.co.uk ☎ 01359 240393

The Walk

1 From the car park turn left to the road junction. For the **Bull Inn** turn right and you'll find the pub in 100 metres on the left. To start the walk turn left at the junction along **Green Road** past **Mill Lane** and at the next junction turn right along **Drinkstone Road** where you will soon find yourself on a country lane. Go gently down to the next junction and turn right, then immediately left

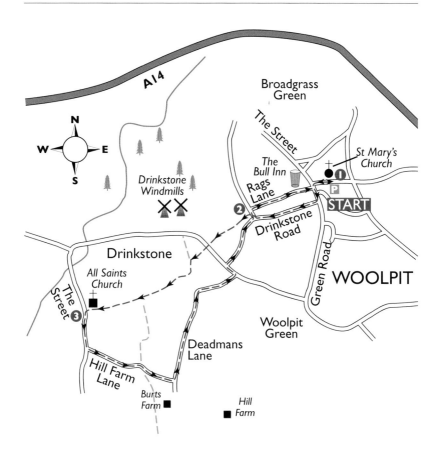

along the footpath. **Drinkstone Windmills** can be seen to your right. Go across the field and cross a brook to the road.

2 Take the footpath almost opposite. At the end of this field, go left through the trees. In 100 metres, at the next footpath junction, turn right along the edge of a field, then diagonally across a crop field. Cross a ditch and continue along the boundary of the next field. At the end of the hedgerow, go left around the field edge then immediately right between two crop fields, going underneath the telegraph wires. Proceed through an area of scrub and greenery to a metal kissing gate which leads into the graveyard of **All Saints Church**. Go past the church with its impressive red brick tower to the lane.

3 Turn left along the lane (**The Street**). When you reach the next road junction, turn left along **Hill Farm Lane**. Proceed all the way to the end of the lane and turn left along **Deadmans Lane**. There is a good distant view of the spire of **Woolpit church**. Continue along the lane for ½ mile, past a seat where you can take a rest. The lane bends right and leads to a road junction where you turn left and then immediately right (to **Woolpit**). This takes you back to the road junction at **Drinkstone Road** you passed at the beginning of the walk. Instead of retracing your steps, turn

left here and then take the next road on the right (**Rags Lane**), passing **Mitre Close** and bungalows and cottages. At the end you are back in **Woolpit** village. Turn left to the **Bull Inn** or right to return to the car park.

Places of Interest

On the walk you will pass through the parish of Drinkstone, and at Rookery Farm there is the unusual spectacle of two windmills side by side. These are known as **Drinkstone Windmills** and were both worked by many generations of the Clover family. The white one (right) is a Grade I listed post mill dating from 1689, making it the oldest windmill in Suffolk. The Grade II listed smock mill next to it was built in 1780.

In 1984 the Woolpit History Group started collecting evidence of the existence of early settlers from the surrounding fields, many of which are on display at **Woolpit & District Museum** in the village. Exhibits are from Roman times to the present day and include pottery, coins, a Victorian kitchen and pieces from the local brick-making works. The Museum is open every Saturday, Sunday and Bank Holiday Monday from 2.00pm to 4.30pm from Easter until the last weekend of September.

Walk 13
HOLBROOK

Distance: 5 miles (8.2 km)

Map: OS Explorer 197 Ipswich, Felixstowe & Harwich.
Grid Ref: TM168366.

How to get there: From the A137 between Ipswich and Brantham, turn onto the B1080 which runs through Holbrook village. Pass All Saints church on your right and take the next left onto The Street. The Village Hall is on the right next to the Methodist Church. **Sat Nav:** IP9 2PZ.

Parking: Holbrook Village Hall car park.

Lakes, rivers and streams abound on this lovely walk from the village of Holbrook. The route circumnavigates the Royal Hospital School with its landmark tower seen from various points along the way. You'll pass a stretch of Alton Water, a large manmade

reservoir with boating and other water activities, stroll along a path overlooking the River Stour, before following the route of a countryside stream on the return to Holbrook village.

THE PUB **THE SWAN** has been serving drinks in Holbrook since 1874. Expect a warm welcome and a good selection of real ales, ciders, lagers and wine.
⊕ facebook.com/theswanpubholbrook ☎ 01473 554030

If you're looking for something to eat, the **KINGS HEAD STUTTON** is just a couple of miles away along the Holbrook Road. The traditional menu is full of locally sourced produce which can be eaten in the restaurant or in the lovely beer garden. Open for food Wednesday to Sunday.
⊕ thekingsheadstutton.co.uk ☎ 01473 328898

The Walk

1 Turn left out of the car park and keep ahead until you reach the main road. Turn right and, keeping to the pavement, walk along **Church Hill** for 300 metres until you reach the church. Just after the fire station, opposite the church, turn right into **Hyams Lane**. Immediately after passing **Five Acres Road** (on the right) take the footpath on the left which runs next to a large crop field. Go down to the end and turn right at the T-junction. Follow the

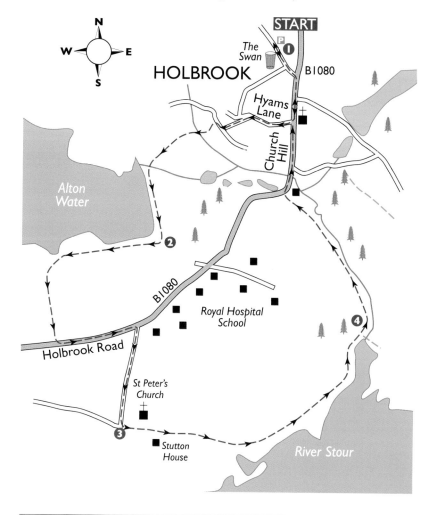

path through the trees for ¼ mile and eventually you emerge out into the open at **Alton Water**. Bear left and follow the path towards the sailing club and the visitor centre. At the end by the wall, turn right.

2 Walk on the grass area between the road and the reservoir. After passing the sailing club car park, head for the pavement and follow the road around to the left past the visitor centre and café. Continue to the end where you reach the main road (**Holbrook Road**). Here you turn left along the walkway. Just as you approach the **Royal Hospital School** buildings, turn right along a shady lane (signed to **The Drift**). Go all the way to the end where you turn left.

3 Continue down past **St Peter's Church** (which is usually open to visitors). Swing left then right following the footpath signs past Grade II listed **Stutton House**. The path narrows then swings right. Cross a bridge and bear left up the bank onto the raised path with views of the **River Stour** to your right. Further along there are also good views to the left of the **Royal Hospital School**. Follow the riverside path for over ½ mile. At the end, where it connects to a gravel track, turn right along the track.

4 At the footpath junction by the metal gate, go straight ahead. Pass through the metal pedestrian gate and out into a grassy meadow. Keep to the left at first but then you bear right across the field (following the footpath sign) to another gate. After passing through, go sharp left onto a path between a fence and the stream, and onto a boardwalk. Continue on to where the route becomes more shaded. The path twists and turns with the stream then turns away left and joins a stony driveway before connecting to the road soon after. Turn right past **The Old Mill** and use the pavement to go uphill. Keep walking up **Church Hill**, retracing your steps and then turning left along **The Street** to return to the **Swan** inn and the car park.

Places of Interest

Alton Water is the largest reservoir in Suffolk. It opened in 1987 to mitigate the water shortage in the Ipswich area and now feeds Ipswich and the villages on the Shotley Peninsular. Today the park hosts activities such as sailing, windsurfing and many other watersports. Fishing, cycling, walking trails and picnic sites are also available.

⊕ anglianwaterparks.co.uk/alton-water

Associated with the Royal Navy, the **Royal Hospital School** is an independent boarding and day school which originally was located at Greenwich but transferred to Holbrook in 1933.

Walk 14

POLSTEAD

Distance: 3 miles (5 km)

Map: OS Explorer 197 Ipswich, Felixstowe & Harwich.
Grid Ref: TL993383.

How to get there: The village of Polstead is two miles south of the A1071 and south-west of Hadleigh, or from the A134, east of Leavenheath. **Sat Nav:** CO6 5AL.

Parking: In the pub car park or there are a few spaces by the green at the front of the pub.

Polstead is a pretty village with thatched cottages and beautiful surrounding countryside. The route heads to the south towards Stoke-by-Nayland with distant views of the village on undulating landscape. You'll walk along the valley of the River Box and along part of the St Edmund Way, then return through attractive woodland.

THE PUB THE COCK INN lies in the centre of the village and is a traditional 17th-century country pub. There is a log fire for colder days and a lovely garden to the front of the pub which overlooks the village green. They serve a selection of real ales, over 30 gins, fine wines and superb, seasonal home-cooked food. Dogs are very welcome.
⊕ thecockinnpolstead.co.uk ☎ 01206 263150

The Walk

1 From the pub entrance, cross to the main road and go right heading downhill along **Polstead Hill** (to **Boxford**). At the road T-junction at the bottom of the hill, next to the lake, take the footpath opposite, by the wooden gate, going up the bank. Go across the meadow past the oak tree. Polstead parish church can be seen to the right. At the other side of the field go through a metal kissing gate and turn right along the lane. Continue past pretty cottages and cross the **River Box**. In 100 metres, just past the junction with **Mill Lane**, take the footpath on the left.

2 Follow the path raised above the floodplain to your left. Keep to the right and after a while go through a metal gate and along by the electric fence. Proceed past the buildings of **Scotland Place Farm** and go through a gate by the converted barn to the road. Turn left along the road. Cross the river and in 100 metres take the footpath on the left, over a footbridge. Pass a lake on the left. There is a seat for a rest overlooking the lake. Go through another gate and at the next path junction bear right across a footbridge. Go through a gate and follow the path uphill between trees to the farm building.

3 At the track junction just after the farm building, turn left leaving the track so that the tall pine trees are on your right. Soon after follow a waymarker going right through the trees on both sides. Pass a picnic table and continue uphill to the road junction. Head straight up the lane and almost immediately take the next footpath on the left through a gap in the hedge. Go across a little meadow. At the bottom, cross three consecutive stiles by the red barn.

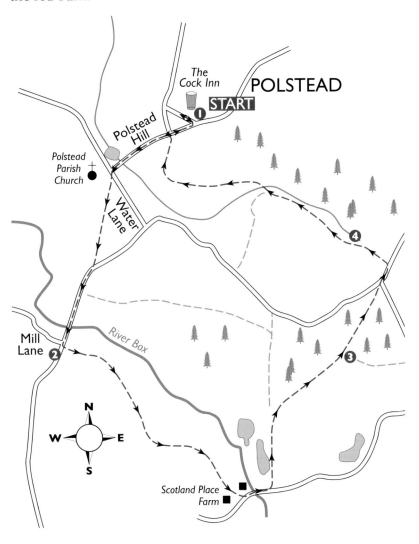

4 Go around a large pond via a gate and across a boardwalk, then up steps and bear right between the fence and a hedge. Continue on past a babbling brook to your right. At the next path junction turn right through a gate. Pass a pond to the right and up through trees. At the next path junction continue straight on through a metal kissing gate into a grassy field. At the end, by the wooden fence, turn right and go up past the end of the cul-de-sac to the road. The pub is to your right.

Places of Interest

The town of **Hadleigh** lies less than 5 miles to the north-east of Polstead. It has 246 timber and brick listed buildings. Most of these buildings can be found in the High Street, some with highly detailed 17th-century plasterwork or 'pargeting' which is a rare trade centred in East Anglia. Originating in the 14th century, **Toppesfield Bridge**, over the River Brett, was widened in 1812 and is the oldest in the county still carrying vehicles.

Walk 15
CHELSWORTH

Distance: 2 or 3¼ miles (3.2 or 5.2 km)

Map: OS Explorer 196 Sudbury, Hadleigh & Dedham Vale. **Grid Ref:** TL982480.

How to get there: From the A1141 between Lavenham and Hadleigh, turn off at Monks Eleigh onto the B1115. This takes you directly into the village of Chelsworth where you'll find the Peacock Inn on the left. **Sat Nav:** IP7 7HU.

Parking: There is a small parking area opposite the pub but you can also park along the road outside.

Suffolk is full of beautiful 'chocolate-box' villages and this walk features two of them. Situated in the heart of the county, the walk starts in Chelsworth, where many of the houses are listed by

English Heritage, before heading to the equally lovely Bildeston and back again. There is an abundance of thatched cottages and Tudor houses with their exposed timbers, mullion windows and jetties (overhangs). This walk is for all ages as there is a shortcut option with no stiles. There are also seats to rest by the church and in Bildeston town square.

THE PUB **THE PEACOCK INN** is the only pub in Chelsworth village (although there are two pubs in Bildeston). It is a freehold pub of character, and dates from the 14th century with old beams and jetties. There are two sections to the pub, a drinking area with a log burner and an eating area with an open fireplace. To one side of the pub is a pleasant garden with outdoor seating.
⊕ thepeacockchelsworth.com ☎ 01449 743952

The Walk

1 From the road junction opposite the pub, head westwards towards **Monks Eleigh** (left if facing the pub). There is a narrow verge on one side, then a pavement on the other. The road bends right, then, as it bends sharp left, opposite the village sign, turn right up a stony track. Pass **Chelsworth Wood** and continue straight ahead going gently uphill into open farmland. Follow alongside a ditch to your right. When this ends turn right.

2 Follow the waymarker going gently uphill between fields. In the corner of the field, bear right across a footbridge and keep right at the junction on the other side. Go up along the field edge with a hedge to the right. Continue along the grass path. At the end of the field go right, joining a farm track taking you to **Church Farm**. The path bends right past the pond and then left to the church. Here you can take the shortcut and turn right at the footpath junction and follow from point 5.

3 To see the village of **Bildeston**, proceed on past the church along **Church Lane**. Pass two seats (resting point) and go downhill along a footway. Go straight on at the road junction (with **Consent Lane**) and into Bildeston village. Go right into **Chapel Street** at the next junction, passing Tudor cottages and go up to the town square. Turn left going past **Duke Street** and the **King's Head** pub. Continue along the main street to the end of the village. After the last house take the footpath on the left over a stile.

4 Go through a meadow of long grass. This gradually bends left to a double stile either side of a footbridge. Proceed up to another stile and footbridge over the stream to the sports field by the lane. Turn left along quiet **Consent Lane**. Just before a black converted barn, take the footpath on the right over a footbridge going up alongside the crop field. At the top you turn left following the footpath bending this way and that back to the church.

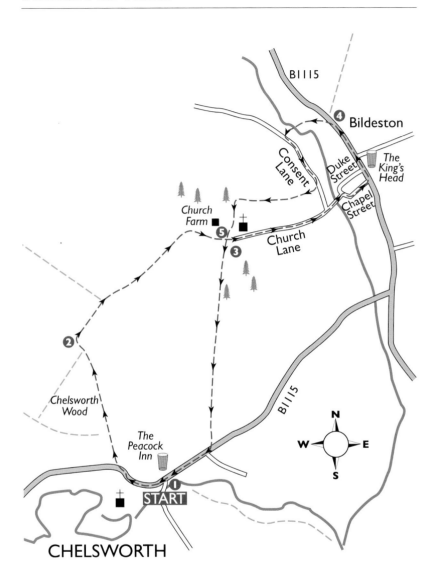

❺ At **Church Lane** take the footpath opposite the church, entering a large field. Follow a grass track. Pass a wood and keep straight on into the next field where there is a good path. There are views to the right with **Monks Eleigh church** in the distance. Go straight on down an open field towards the village. At the road turn right and keep to the verge on the other side. After a few minutes you are back at the road junction by the **Peacock Inn**.

Places of Interest

Less than a mile to the west, between Chelsworth and the pretty village of Monks Eleigh, is **Bridge Farm Barns**. Open every day with free parking, there are craft shops, antiques, vintage and collectables, a picture gallery displaying works by local artists and a tearoom. It is also the home of **Lavenham Falconry** which has a large collection of owls and other birds of prey. They offer a hands-on experience to visitors and my own family enjoyed a session learning about flying and feeding the birds.

Walk 16
LAVENHAM

Distance: 5¼ miles (8.4 km)

Map: OS Explorer 196 Sudbury, Hadleigh & Dedham Vale.
Grid Ref: TL914489.

How to get there: Lavenham is situated on the A1141 between Hadleigh and the A134 to Bury St Edmunds. Church Street begins at the junction of the High Street and Water Street. The pub and car park are on the left, opposite the church. Sat Nav: CO10 9SA.

Parking: The free car park off Church Street next to the Cock Horse Inn.

Lavenham is one of the best-preserved medieval towns in England with over 300 buildings of historic interest. Many of the surviving timber-framed buildings were built during the 15th and 16th centuries when the town became wealthy from the cloth trade and were the homes of rich wool merchants. This route takes the walker to the neighbouring village of Brent Eleigh and back again into the heart of Lavenham town.

THE PUB THE COCK HORSE INN, located on the edge of the town, is one of a number of pubs in Lavenham. It has a welcoming atmosphere and serves traditional home-cooked classics. There is outside seating to the front, a dog friendly bar and a restaurant. Open every day from 11am apart from Mondays.
⊕ thecockhorse.com ☎ 01787 827330

The Walk

1 Turn right out of the car park. Walk down the main street (**Church Street**) and take the first turning on the right into **Bear's Lane**. Continue for ¾ mile, all the way to the end; the lane narrows into a quiet country lane and passes **Weaners Farm** and **Peg Weasel Farm**. When you reach **Bear's Lane Farm** go left between the hedge and the fence. It bends one way and the other and out into an open field to your right, at the end of which, you turn right the other side of the hedge, going down a dusty track.

2 At the bottom it crosses a ditch and swings left. At the next junction take the track on the left, then almost immediately bear right onto a narrow grass path that runs parallel with the brook to your left. Proceed for 300 metres then pass through a shady wood. When you get to the track that crosses the path, take the footpath through the hedge almost opposite (slightly to the right). Pass a lake on your left. At the end of the lake go right across a concealed ditch then continue to your left alongside a crop field. At the end you reach a lane (**Cock Lane**).

3 Turn left over the bridge and proceed along the lane until you reach the main road (A1141) and the **Cock Inn**. Cross with care and take the road opposite. At the next junction in 200 metres, go left, crossing the road bridge and then heading uphill, passing **St Mary's church**. At the next junction, go straight on (towards **Preston**). As the lane bends sharp right, take the tree-lined bridleway on the left. Continue on past **Spragg's Wood** and keep on this path for 1¼ miles. When you eventually reach **Clayhill Farm**, the path converts to a lane.

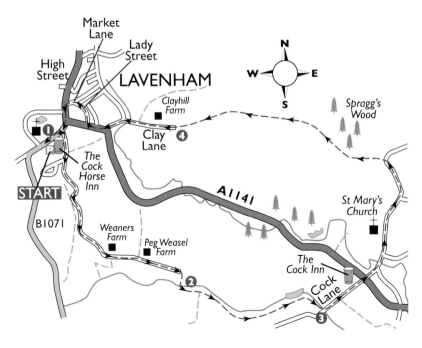

4 Continue to **Brett Farm** where you cross a bridge and at the road junction turn left. At the next junction in 100 metres, turn right into **Water Lane** with its magnificent Tudor buildings. Take the third turning on the right into **Lady Street**. This leads up to the main square with the **Guildhall**, museum and shops. Leave by **Market Lane** taking you back down to the **High Street** where you turn left along the High Street. Head uphill into **Church Street** to the car park on the left where you started.

Places of Interest

The 15th-century **Lavenham Guildhall** in Market Place is Grade I listed and is in the possession of the National Trust. It is open all year round and there is a permanent exhibition cataloguing the growth of the cloth trade in Lavenham. Next to it is the attractive and even older, late 14th-century **Little Hall Museum** which tells the story of the town. It has a walled garden and holds a programme of special events throughout the year. The magnificent **Church of St Peter and St Paul**, near the start of the walk, is also worth a visit. It is open daily and is one of the most visited churches in East Anglia.

Walk 17
GREAT WRATTING

Distance: 4 miles (6.8 km)

Map: OS Explorer 210 Newmarket & Haverhill.
Grid Ref: TL691481.

How to get there: Great Wratting is on the B1061 between Kedington and Great Thurlow. The Red Lion is on the main road ½ mile north of the junction with the A143. Sat Nav: CB9 7HA.

Parking: In the large car park at the Red Lion.

This tranquil walk takes you through some wonderful rolling countryside and includes the village of Kedington as well as Great Wratting, where you'll find the river teeming with crayfish and some attractive thatched cottages, some dating back to the 16th century. The route begins along the Stour Valley Path to Kedington and then heads westwards towards Haverhill and up to a plateau where there are amazing views of the surrounding countryside.

THE PUB THE RED LION is an early 19th-century, family-run country pub with a friendly atmosphere. There is good choice of food with a seven day à la carte menu plus snacks and vegetarian options. The pub is dog friendly, and on a warm day there is an extensive, pleasant garden to sit in with a children's play area. If visiting on a cold day there is a nice log fire inside the pub.
⊕ facebook.com/wrattingredlion ☎ 01440 783237

The Walk

1 From the pub go right along the road. At the village sign, turn right and then right again into **The Street**. Pass over the bridge by the ford crossing the **River Stour** and, after passing some pretty thatched cottages and the property called **High Gables**, turn right onto a narrow footpath. Head straight across the field and, on the other side, bear left along the field edge to reach the far corner. Follow the footpath arrow right into the next field. Go left around the fallen ash tree, then over a bridge and through a gate into the next field. Go straight across, through another gate and then a stile to the main road.

2 Go straight over with care and cross a little brook by the cottage and along the field edge to a shady wood. Cross a brook into a

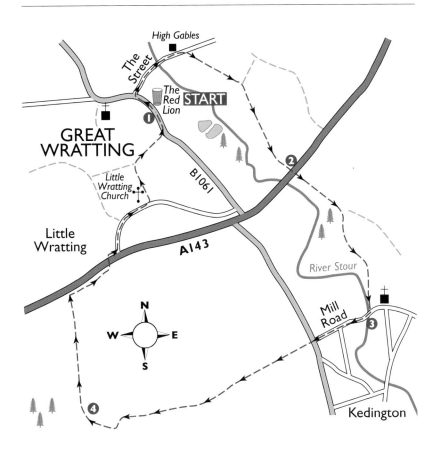

field and go right. Look out for a footpath turning immediately right, back across the brook. Follow the field edge but then bear left across the field following the telegraph poles. At the telegraph post junction, veer right towards the church tower. At the corner of the field the footpath continues past the church down a shady path to the road.

❸ Turn right along the road over the river by the old mill. Proceed along the pavement and up to the T-junction. Turn left then immediately right along a footpath. As the dusty track veers left you go straight on uphill under the telegraph wires. As you climb higher there are magnificent views of the surrounding countryside. Cross a footbridge and continue straight on for

½ mile until you reach a farm. Here you veer left along the track and then immediately turn right along a concrete track just past the wooden barn. Pass the partly concealed moat on the left to a little T-junction at the bottom.

4 Turn right onto the long straight tarmac track and walk all the way to the end. Turn right along the little access road that runs parallel with the main road, the A143. At the end, where it connects to the main road, carefully cross over and turn right. In 100 metres turn left down the lane to **Little Wratting church**, passing cottages and houses. Immediately past the church, turn left onto a footpath. Go gently downhill and after crossing a ditch turn right. Proceed down to the end of the field where you descend the bank to the road. Turn left along the pavement and the **Red Lion** is a little further along on the right.

Places of Interest

About 4 miles east of Great Wratting is the popular little town of **Clare** with its antique shops, quaint houses and pubs. You'll find the remains of an **Augustinian Priory** which is worth a visit and a museum depicting rural life in bygone Suffolk. There is also a country park by the old railway with a visitor centre and an old Norman castle mound or motte, which you can climb to the top of.

Walk 18
CHEVINGTON

Distance: 3¼ miles (5.1 km)

Map: OS Explorer 211 Bury St Edmunds. **Grid Ref:** TL783593.

How to get there: From the A143 between Bury St Edmunds and Haverhill, take the turning off north towards Chedburgh. Drive through the village and in 1¼ miles you'll reach the centre of Chevington, where you'll find the Greyhound on your left. Sat Nav: IP29 5QS.

Parking: The large car park at the Greyhound.

This walk takes you across open farmland and along quiet lanes around the small village of Chevington, via the parish of Hargrave. The village was founded on the site of a Saxon camp and was given over to the Abbey of St Edmund after the Norman Conquest. Chevington Hall was once a retreat house for the Abbots and the local woods were used by them for hunting deer and fishing.

THE PUB THE GREYHOUND, dating from about 1725, is the only pub in the village. It has a friendly atmosphere and has been run by the same family for the past 25 years. It specializes in Indian food but has other choices on the menu, including burgers and fish and chips. There are no fewer than three log burners inside, and there is a large garden for warmer days. Open every day except Monday.

🌐 facebook.com/thegreyhoundchevington ☎ 01284 850765

The Walk

1 Turn left out of the pub car park and walk along the lane for 200 metres. Take the first footpath on the left running alongside a fence. Continue along this grass path between fences, crossing a track and then a ditch. Carry on through a field and then straight on into the next field. Head through trees to a path junction where you turn right, going gently downhill following a high hedge to your left. After crossing a little concrete bridge at the bottom, bear right. Follow a wide track keeping right of the large oak tree. At the next path junction, turn right for ¼ mile to reach the road.

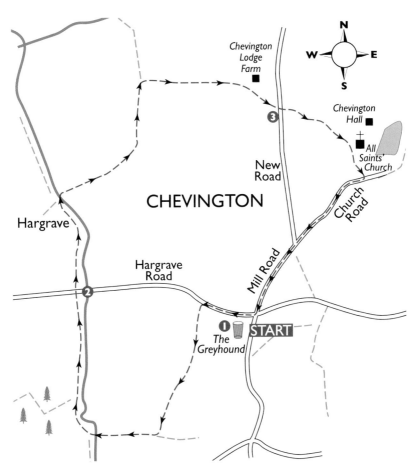

2 Cross over and just to the right take the footpath through the hedge. Follow the field edge round to the right, along by a deep ditch. At the end of the field keep right and cross a bridge over the stream. Follow the left edge of the field going uphill. Half way along the field, turn right onto a footpath cutting across the crop field. Cross a bridge and go straight on across the next large field, passing **Chevington Lodge Farm** to your left. Proceed down to the road (**New Road**).

3 Cross over and take the footpath opposite. Follow along by a fence going sharp right at the end of the field. Cross a stile

into a meadow. Cross another stile to the left and head into the churchyard (usually open to the public). **Chevington Hall** is just beyond the church. Go past the church entrance and down to the lane. Turn right along **Church Road**. At the road junction bear left along **Mill Road** which brings you to the crossroads with the **Greyhound** opposite.

Places of Interest

Just a few miles north-east of Chevington is the National Trust's **Ickworth House**, easily recognised by its impressive domed rotunda. The estate was created by the Hervey family who acquired the land in 1432 but work on the current building wasn't started until 1795. Ickworth remained in the family until, in 1956, the estate was handed over to the Treasury in lieu of death duties and was then subsequently given to the National Trust. Inside there are some impressive statues, a fine collection of silverware and fine works of art, including pieces by Gainsborough. Taking up the east wing is the Ickworth Hotel and the west wing has more recently been renovated into a conference centre and restaurant.

Walk 19
DALHAM

Distance: 3 or 5 miles (5 or 8 km)

Map: OS Explorer 210 Newmarket & Haverhill.
Grid Ref: TL722616.

How to get there: Dalham lies on the B1085. It can be reached from the A14, turning off at Kentford onto the B1085 and going through Moulton to the village. **Sat Nav:** CB8 8TG.

Parking: Roadside in front of the Affleck Arms by the river.

This is a quiet walk in a rural backwater of western Suffolk in the pretty village of Dalham with its many thatched cottages. The village has a windmill, Lower Mill, which you pass at the beginning of your journey and is a landmark which can be seen from various points along the route. The pub gets its name from the Affleck family, who lived at Dalham Hall for 200 years. You will pass the house and their obelisk monument in the churchyard on the route. The walk briefly runs into the parish of Ashley in Cambridgeshire before returning into Suffolk via the River Kennett.

THE PUB

THE AFFLECK ARMS is a friendly, family-run pub. It is deceptively large with four linking bar areas, one with a log burner for colder days. There is also seating outside both to the front and back. Opening hours are limited during the week when the pub does not open until 5pm. It is cash only.
☎ 01638 500306

If you require food on a weekday, MOULTON STORES & POST OFFICE in the next village has a tearoom and sells snacks and drinks. Alternatively, try the RED LION in Cheveley, 3 miles away. On offer are daily specials and a seasonal menu.
☎ 01638 730233

The Walk

1 Turn left out of the pub car park and go up **Stores Hill**. On the left towards the top you pass **Dalham windmill**. At the next road junction take the footpath that commences from between the two roads, running uphill with a hedge to your right. There are wonderful distant views to the left. In the corner of the field, go up the bank to the right and continue along the field edge. Go

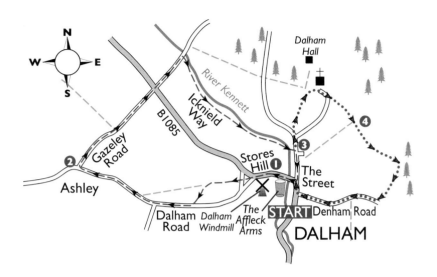

through a gap in the hedge. Here the true line of the footpath straight across the field may not be possible so go left around the field edge and then turn right at the corner, parallel with the lane. When you reach the hedge, go out left onto the lane (**Dalham Road**). Turn right and go gently downhill for ½ mile until you reach the road junction at **Ashley**.

2 Turn right along **Gazeley Road**. Proceed downhill for just over ½ mile to the crossroads. Cross over and keep straight down a tree-lined lane. In 300 metres, at the bottom of the hill and just before the bridge, turn right onto a footpath. This is part of the **Icknield Way**. The route runs along a wide grass track on the field edge and parallel with the **River Kennett** for almost 1 mile. The windmill can be seen towards the end. You enter a wooded area around a stile and in 100 metres you cross a bridge to the road.

For a shortcut you can turn right along the road (**The Street**) which will take you directly back to the pub within around 5 minutes.

3 For the extended walk, turn left along the lane, passing some pretty cottages. Once past **Church Lane**, take the footpath through the kissing gate on the right going gently uphill between rows of horse chestnut trees. This takes you to the church and **Dalham Hall**. Turn right along the track. At the fork keep left along the private road and continue along the concrete track until you pass **Garden House** where you go straight on with the path converting to an unmade track.

4 The path descends through the trees. Cross a brook and start going back uphill. At the junction, turn right and follow the circular walk waymarker through the trees. At the next fork keep right along the footpath still through a wooded area. The windmill can be seen to the right. Proceed down to the lane (**Denham Road**) and turn right. Continue for ½ mile back to the village. At the T-junction, turn right to the **Affleck Arms**.

Places of Interest

The **Lower Mill** in Dalham is a three-storey smock mill built in the last decade of the 18th century. It worked as a flour mill until 1926 when production ceased and it began to fall into disrepair. The mill was bought in 1972 by Frank Farrow and, with the help of grants, restoration work began. It currently doesn't have its sails but retains its three pairs of millstones which rest on a very unusual hurst frame above the level of the first floor.

Walk 20
BARTON MILLS

Distance: 3 miles (5 km)

Map: OS Explorer 226 Ely & Newmarket. **Grid Ref:** TL724738.

How to get there: From the A11 between Newmarket and Thetford, take the Barton Mills turning, just south of the roundabout where the A11 meets the A1065 and the A1101. Turn right into Chestnut Close and the Bull Inn is at the end on the left. **Sat Nav:** IP28 6AA.

Parking: In the car park at the Bull Inn, but please ask permission before you set out.

Barton Mills is a village just to the south of Mildenhall. Alexander Fleming, the famous physician and microbiologist who discovered penicillin, had a holiday home in the main street. Rather unusually, the village is also the host of an annual two-day scarecrow festival and holds a Guinness World Record for the most scarecrows ever built at any one time. The walk takes you along the pretty River Lark to the market town of Mildenhall and back through Barton Mills village.

THE PUB **THE BULL INN** is a hotel and restaurant as well as a pub. Originally a 17th-century coaching inn, it was a popular stopping place for those travelling from London to Norwich or King's Lynn. Its famous visitors include Lloyd George, Queen Victoria and allegedly, Queen Elizabeth I. Today, it has a large bar area, a good-sized restaurant and outside seating areas to the front and back. Opening for breakfast at 7.30am, food is served all day, every day.

⊕ bullinn-bartonmills.com ☎ 01638 711001

The Walk

1 From the main entrance of the pub, take the cul-de-sac opposite (**Old Mill Lane**) which immediately bends left, crossing the **River Lark**. On the other side of the road bridge, turn left down steps onto a footpath which follows the north bank of the river. There is an information board on the river bank. Continue along the river path for 1 mile. **Mildenhall church tower** comes into view. Go past the footbridge over the river and then the path bends right, away from the river, passing **Sainsbury's** and the **Tourist Information Centre** to the little **Mildenhall & District Museum**.

2 Just past the museum, turn left along **Market Street**. At the end, turn left. Pass the 14th-century church entrance and take the path immediately on the right, running alongside the church. Go left at the end along **Aldrych Place** taking you back to the high street (**Mill Street**). Turn right along the pavement. The road bends right and crosses the river. At the road junction take the left turn down **Station Road** (to **Barton Mills**). Follow the pavement and when this runs out continue ahead along the lane. Where the road bends sharp left, keep straight on along a footpath which is a hard-surfaced private access drive to **Grange Farm**.

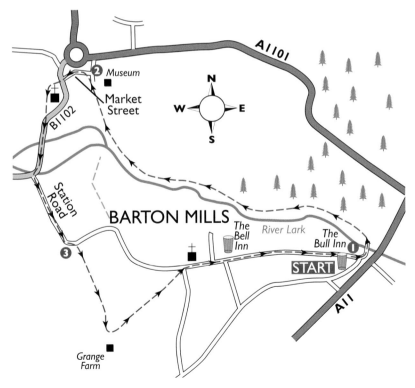

3 Follow the hedge-line for 400 metres. Where the path enters the farm, keep straight on into the trees. By the metal gate, turn left onto a footpath bordered by trees to the right. Go around a metal gate at the end of the field and onto a hard-surfaced track past houses and then the village green and recreation ground. When you reach the road junction by the church, bear right along **The Street**. Pass the **Bell inn**, a converted chapel and, further along, a beautiful thatched cottage. At the end, on the corner, you are back at the **Bull Inn**.

Places of Interest

Mildenhall is a small market town situated in the north-west corner of Suffolk. The museum in the centre of the town, which you pass on the walk, contains displays of local history and wildlife, along with the history of the RAF bases at Mildenhall and Lakenheath, and information on the **Mildenhall Treasure**. Discovered in 1942, the Mildenhall Treasure is a hoard of Roman silver tableware dating from the 4th century which is now on display in the British Museum. Entrance to Mildenhall & District Museum is free. ⊕ mildenhallmuseum.co.uk.

OTHER TITLES FROM COUNTRYSIDE BOOKS

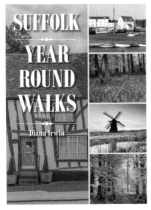

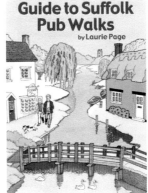

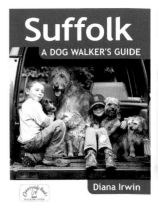

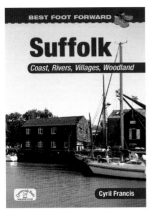

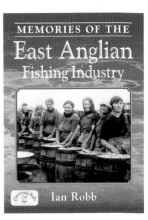

To see the full range of books by Countryside Books please visit
www.countrysidebooks.co.uk

Follow us on   @CountrysideBooks